DATE DUE

SPORTS SKILLS
FOR
BOYS AND GIRLS

By

JAMES H. HUMPHREY

Professor of Physical Education
University of Maryland
College Park, Maryland

and

JOY N. HUMPHREY

Instructor
Prince George's County
Maryland Public Schools

Illustrations by

Fred J. Altiere

CHARLES C THOMAS • PUBLISHER
Springfield • Illinois • U.S.A.

Published and Distributed Throughout the World by
CHARLES C THOMAS • PUBLISHER
Bannerstone House
301-327 East Lawrence Avenue, Springfield, Illinois, U.S.A.

© *1980, by* CHARLES C THOMAS • PUBLISHER
ISBN 0-398-04027-3
Library of Congress Catalog Card Number: 79-24538

Printed in the United States of America
V-R-1

Library of Congress Cataloging in Publication Data

Humphrey, James Harry, 1911-
  Sports skills for boys and girls.

  Includes index.
  1. Physical education for children. 2. Sports for
children. I. Humphrey, Joy M., joint author.
II. Title.
GV443.H83   613.7′042   79-24538
ISBN 0-398-04027-3

A MESSAGE FOR YOU

THIS book has been written for boys and girls nine to twelve years of age. This is a time in their lives when many boys and girls begin to get very interested in sports. It is important for you to learn how to do the skills in the right way. If you learn to do this you will have much more success as a player. Also it will be more fun for you. Here are some things to remember as you try to learn the skills.

1. Many of the sports skills are alike. They are based on ideas of how to move the body, and how to move and receive a ball.
2. Skills should be learned correctly from the beginning. If you learn to do a skill the wrong way it might become a habit. Sometimes these habits are hard to break.
3. Skills must be practiced. This is the only way you will perform them better.
4. You do not have to be perfect in a skill before you use it in a game. Playing in games helps you improve on your skills.

At one time it was thought that sports were mainly for boys. This is no longer true. Many girls like to improve their skills. They enjoy playing games where the skills are used. All of the skills and games in this book can be engaged in by both boys and girls. Boys may want to play together by themselves. The same is true as far as girls are concerned. Sometimes they might like to play in the games together. The main thing is, whether they play together or separately, both boys and girls can learn the skills.

We hope you enjoy the book and that you will learn a lot about how to do the skills.

CONTENTS

Contents ix

SPORTS SKILLS
FOR
BOYS AND GIRLS

Chapter 1

SKILLS THAT MOVE THE BODY

AS you know, you move your body every day in many different ways. When we talk about skill we are thinking about how well a certain body movement is done. There are certain things you can do in body movements to help you move better. These body movements are what we are concerned with in this chapter.

An important thing to remember is that not all of you will start out being highly skilled in your body movements. However, most all of you will be able to perform better if you follow certain suggestions that can make you move your body better. We want to talk about those ways you can move your body so that you will be able to play better in games that require different kinds of body movements. The skills to move the body that we will explain are *walking, running, leaping, jumping, hopping, galloping* and *sliding*. Maybe you have not heard of all these skills, but all of them are important in some way. If you learn how to do them the best you can, then you should do better in those games where these skills are needed.

WALKING

You may wonder why we take the time to explain the skill *walking*. The reason is that walking is the most basic skill you use as you move about. Learning to walk in the proper way can help you perform other movement skills well.

Walking is transferring the weight from one foot to the other. The walk is started with a push-off backward against the ground with the ball and toes of the foot. The ball of the foot is the part just in back of the toes. After this first movement, the leg swings forward from the hip. The heel of the other foot is placed down, the outer half of the foot next, and then the next push-off is made with the toes pointing straight ahead. You

3

Figure 1. WALKING!

continue by putting one foot in front of the other this way. The arms are swung at the sides freely. The left arm swings forward as the right foot moves forward, and the right arm swings forward as the left foot moves forward. This means that you swing the opposite arm with the leading foot. If you practice walking in this way, it should make it easier for you to do other skills that move the body.

Some Things to Try in Walking

1. Walk along and try to keep your body straight.
2. Walk forward, sideward, and backward.
3. Try walking with the toes turned in, then with the toes turned out. You will see how much better it is with the toes pointed straight ahead.
4. Walk along with a change in speed. First walk slow and then speed up and walk faster — go from slow to fast and from fast to slow.
5. Walk raising the knees high.
6. Walk without bending your knees.
7. Walk slowly with very short steps and then fast with very long steps.
8. Walk fast with very short steps and then slowly with very long steps.
9. Walk along with one or more people and see how well you stay in step.

RUNNING

As in walking, running is transferring the weight from one foot to the other. However, the weight is transferred with much more speed. The ball of the foot touches the ground first, and the toes point straight ahead. There is a short time when the body is in the air with no contact with the ground. This is different from the walk in which there is always contact with the ground with one of the feet.

In the run there is more bending at the knee; this means lifting the leg higher. There is also a higher lifting of the arm and bending at the elbow. In running there is more of a forward body lean than there is in walking; again, the head points straight ahead. Sometimes boys and girls who have not been taught to run in the right way will do certain things wrong. Some will use a backward rather than a forward lean of the body. Others will carry the arms too high and run with the head to the side rather than pointing straight ahead. If you notice that you are making any of these mistakes in running,

Figure 2. RUNNING!

try to correct them at once. Remember that running is the skill that is probably used the most in sports, so you want to try to do your best when you practice it.

Some Things to Try in Running

1. Run in place.
2. Run straight ahead for a short distance as fast as you can.

3. Line up some lawn chairs or other objects and run around and between them.
4. Run to a point and stop; turn and run back.
5. With some friends, practice running while trying to keep out of each other's way.
6. Run for a distance; first fast and then slow.
7. Run along throwing a ball into the air and catching it.
8. Run along with a partner.

LEAPING

Leaping is like a slow run with one important difference: the push-off is up and then forward, with a feeling of "up and over." The landing should be on the ball of the foot with enough bending at the knee so that there is less shock.

Although leaping is not used very much as a special skill for moving the body, there are reasons it is important to learn how to do it. For example, the leap can be used when running to leap over an object. Let us say that you are playing a game, and a player has fallen down in the direction you are running. You can leap over the person rather than running into him. Leaping is also important when you are trying to catch a ball that has been hit or thrown high. A leap for the ball can help you catch it "on the run" so you can keep on moving.

Some Things to Try in Leaping

1. Run along, then leap with one foot and then the other foot.
2. Put something in front of you and then run and leap over it. You can use a small box, but make sure it is low enough so that you can leap over it.
3. Put up several small boxes and run and leap over them first with one foot and then the other.
4. Do five or six leaps without any running steps in between.

Figure 3. LEAPING!

JUMPING

In a way, jumping is like walking and running, as far as the way you move is concerned. A difference is that jumping requires that you get the body higher off the ground. More strength and force is needed for this movement.

We usually think of two ways to jump: one way is to push off on both feet and land on both feet — start with your feet close together and when you land both feet are still close together. Another kind of jump is taking off on one foot and landing on both feet. As in leaping, the landing is on the ball of the foot. Again there should be bending at the knees so that there is less shock. Many sports require good jumping for success. In fact, most any sport that you can name is concerned in some way with jumping.

Some Things to Try in Jumping

1. Stand in place and jump; go just a little bit higher each time.
2. Jump and take a little bit of a turn before you land.
3. Jump forward, sideward, and backward.
4. Make some circles or squares on the ground; jump from one to the other.
5. Get close to a wall and jump. Stretch your arm up high and remember where your fingers are. Now jump and touch the wall. Measure the distance between the fingers when standing and after the jump.
6. Put up some small boxes and jump over them.
7. Hold hands facing a partner: jump up and down while doing so.
8. Have two friends swing a rope while you jump over it.
9. Run a short distance to a line and jump — be sure you have a soft landing place.

HOPPING

In hopping, you take off with one foot and land on that same foot. Jumping is probably easier than hopping because in hopping the body is raised from the ground with only one foot. More strength and force is needed for the hop than the jump. Also, it is harder to balance when doing the hop. To show what we mean by balancing, you can carry out the following action. Stand straight with feet slightly apart. Raise one foot off the ground. You will find that you have to shift your weight over to the other foot right away; if you don't, you will be off balance and will fall down.

Hopping as a skill is not used for sports activities: you are not going to be moving around on only one foot. Even though this is true, hopping is a very important skill to learn. The reason for its importance is that it can help you keep your balance. Let us say that you are playing in a game and you have just "lost your footing." This can happen when you stumble over something or have someone bump into your leg. This means that you cannot use this foot and leg at the time, so you only have one foot to move on. You can take a hop on the other foot and keep your balance. We can show what we mean if you will try this. Walk along slowly and pretend that you have stumbled over something — you can do this by using one foot to kick the other foot lightly — now you have just one foot to move. If you don't move it you will fall forward. If you do hop on it you can stay up until the other foot can be moved forward.

Some Things to Try in Hopping

1. See how long you can stand on one foot.
2. See how long you can stand on the other foot.
3. Hop in place, first on one foot and then the other.
4. Hop and take a short turn.
5. Hop forward.
6. Hop sideward.
7. Hop backward.
8. Hop a short distance on one foot and back on the other foot.
9. Hop over a small box.

GALLOPING

The skill of galloping can be explained by pretending that one foot is hurt. A step is taken with either foot, which is called the *lead* foot. The foot that you are pretending is hurt can bear very little weight. It is brought up only behind the lead foot but not ahead of it. A transfer of weight is then made to the lead foot. A fast limp is really a gallop.

Galloping is a skill that does not have a great deal of use as a means of moving the body. However, it is a very important skill for you to learn. The main reason galloping is important is that it can help you change direction quickly from front to back. Try to gallop forward and then backward to see how quickly you can make the change. When you use the gallop to make this move you can do it much faster. This means that when you can make this kind of change quickly you will have more success in games where it is important to make this quick change.

Some Things to Try in Galloping

1. Gallop forward for a short distance and stop quickly.
2. Gallop backward. You have to do this more slowly because you can't see where you are going. Remember that you start backward with the lead foot.
3. Take about three gallops and then change your lead foot. You do this by taking a step with the trailing foot and making it the lead foot.
4. Gallop and see how close you can stay to the ground.
5. Gallop and see how high you can get. You will find that it is better to stay close to the ground.

SLIDING

Sliding is much the same as galloping. The difference is that the movement is made in a sideward direction. In galloping, the movement is made forward or backward. In sliding, one of the feet, which is the lead foot, is placed out to the side. The other foot is drawn up to it. The weight is shifted to the lead foot and back to the drawing foot. Try to slide by doing the following movements: stand straight with feet slightly apart; place one foot out to the side and bring the other foot up to it. Keep doing this to the same side and then change and go the other way.

Sliding is another skill that is not used very much to move the body. However, like hopping and galloping, it is a very important skill to learn. Sliding helps you move from side to side very quickly. When you learn how to slide well you do not have to cross your feet to go from side to side. There are many games where this skill is needed for success in the game. This is true in the game of basketball when you are guarding another player. You have to be able to slide back and forth quickly if you are going to do a good job of guarding the other player.

Some Things to Try in Sliding

1. Slide in one direction very slowly.
2. Slide in the other direction as quickly as you can.
3. Slide and see how quickly you can stop and slide the other way.
4. Slide and keep low to the ground.
5. Slide and raise yourself high off the ground — see how much better it is to keep close to the ground.
6. Get a partner and take his hands; try to slide together.
7. Slide with your partner without holding hands; see if you can stay close together as you face each other.
8. Get several friends and make a circle; join hands and slide one way in the circle and then the other way.

Chapter 2

HELPING SKILLS

MANY people think only of sports skills that require moving the body or throwing or catching a ball. There are other skills that you do not hear much about, but they are important for success in most all sports. We call these *helping skills*. The helping skills that we will talk about here are *starting, stopping, dodging, pivoting, landing,* and *falling.*

STARTING

There are many sports where it is important to know how to get started quickly. Most sports require running, starting, and stopping during the game.

How good a person will be in the skill of starting depends on two things: one of these is called *reaction time,* and the other is called *speed of movement.* Reaction time means how quickly you react after you get a signal. Let us say that you are standing. Another person gives you a signal by saying, "Go!" Reaction time is how long it takes you to start the first move after you hear the signal. Speed of movement is how long it takes you to make the first move after you hear the signal. Again, let us say that you are standing. Another person gives you a signal. Speed of movement is how long it takes for you to move your foot after you hear the signal.

Some Ways to Practice Starting

1. Get a friend for a partner. Stand facing each other a short distance apart: have your feet close together. At a signal from your partner, move your foot out to the side about twelve inches. See how fast you react. See how fast you move your foot. Change, and you give the signal to your partner. Try giving a signal by sound, such as calling, "Go!" Also give a signal by sight by waving an arm as the signal to start. See if

13

it takes longer to start with the sound signal or the sight signal.
2. Start to run as fast as you can. Then start to run in slow motion. You can then see the difference between a fast start and a slow start.

STOPPING

We have already said that many games require running, starting, and stopping during play. Basketball is an example of such a game. You will have much more success in basketball and other games as well if you learn how to stop quickly.

There are two ways of stopping: one of the ways is called the *stride* stop, and the other way is called the *skip* stop. The stride stop is used when you are running along slowly and just stop in stride. Some people call it "stopping in your tracks." When you stop, you bend your knees and lean back a little bit. The reason for these movements is that you will not lose your balance. Try running along slowly and stop with one foot in front and the other behind.

The skip stop is harder to do and also harder to explain. This way of stopping is used when you are making a fast movement and must come to a quick stop. As you are running along the first thing you do is take a little hop on either foot. The other foot touches the ground at just about the same time. It looks like you are landing on both feet at the same time. However, one foot touches the ground slightly ahead of the other. Because it seems that both feet land at the same time, some people call this a jump stop.

Try the skip stop: run along at fairly good speed; take a hop on one foot and bring the other foot down nearly at the same time. Skip stopping takes much practice because you have to be able to judge how fast you are running. Try to do a stride stop while running fast and you will probably find that you will fall forward. The reason for this forward fall is that the stride stop should be used with a slow run.

Some Ways to Practice Stopping

1. Run along and stop.

2. Run along and have someone give you a signal to stop. Have them give you a signal to start and then stop again.
3. Run to a wall and stop just before you get there. See if you did a good job of judging when to stop.
4. Run around and keep changing directions. Have someone give you a signal of when to stop and when to start again.
5. Get some friends and play the game "Start and Stop." In this game several players stand in a line side by side. One person is chosen to be the leader and stands at a goal line some distance away; the leader calls, "Start!" On this signal the players all run forward. The leader calls, "Stop!" Anyone moving after this signal must return to the starting line. This game can go on until one player has reached the goal line. This player can be the leader for the next game. Play the game the same way but use a sight signal rather than a sound signal. The leader can signal by waving the arm or a piece of cloth.

DODGING

In dodging you change the direction of your body while running. To dodge, you stop running forward and change direction. In order to do this body movement, you bend the knees and transfer the weight in the dodging direction: if you are dodging to the right you bend the right knee and transfer the weight of the body to the right foot. You do just the opposite if you want to dodge to the left. After a dodge is made, you can go on in the same direction. This is done by pushing off with the foot where the weight was transferred. The dodge is very important in games where it is necessary to get away from a player of the other team. For example, in basketball it is important to be able to dodge around the person who is guarding you.

Some Ways to Practice Dodging

1. Run up to a certain point and change direction by dodging.
2. Set up several objects and dodge around them.
3. Get a partner; run up to him and then dodge around him.
4. Play a game of tag with some friends and see how important

Figure 4. DODGING!

it is to be able to dodge.

5. Have someone toss a ball at you and try to dodge it.

PIVOTING

Dodging is used to change direction during body movement. Pivoting is used to change direction while the body is not moving. In pivoting, one foot is always kept in place on the ground. The other foot is used to push off. You can turn in any direction, but remember to keep one foot on the ground. The weight of the body is on the foot that stays on the ground. The longest distance you should ever have to pivot is one-half way around. If you have to go more than half way, you should use the other foot as the pivot foot.

Pivoting is important in games where quick movement is necessary but where you are not allowed to move the body. This is very true in basketball where you try to pivot away from the person guarding you. In this way you can have more success in keeping the ball away from him.

Figure 5. PIVOTING!

Some Ways to Practice Pivoting

1. Get a partner: pivot when he calls out a signal.
2. Face your partner and practice pivoting away from him.

3. Run to a point, stop and pivot, and then run back.
4. Have a partner throw a ball to you. When you catch it, make a pivot and protect the ball.
5. Pivot on one foot and then the other. Do this several times.

LANDING

Landing means that the body comes to the ground from a height or distance. One of the most important things to remember in landing is to make the shock less: bend the knees; keep the weight on the balls of the feet; and bend the ankles. After landing, you come to an upright position. The arms are placed out to the side so that you can keep your balance. Many games require you to leave the ground or floor, and this means that you must come down and land. You want to do it in such a way that you will not hurt yourself. Basketball, volleyball, and flag football are games where knowing how to land is important.

Some Ways to Practice Landing

1. Take a short jump into the air and land — remember how we explained landing above.
2. Jump into the air and land; repeat this several times.
3. Take a short slow run, jump, and land.
4. Jump from a short height such as a bench or a chair.

FALLING

You may wonder why we even talk about falling. We all know that in most games we are supposed to stay in an upright position and try not to fall. In spite of this, sometimes a player will lose his balance and fall to the floor or ground. If you know how to fall, there is a much smaller chance of hurting yourself.

Whenever possible a fall should be taken in a way that will keep you from hurting yourself. One way to do this is to try to "break the fall." You can help break your fall with your hands.

t is also important to try to relax or make yourself "go limp."
We sometimes call this "bunching up" when you see that you
are going to fall. You can bunch your body up if you try to get
your arms and legs in close to you.

Some Ways to Practice Falling

1. Get a soft place and roll around in a curled up position.
2. Pretend you are a ball and roll around on a soft place.
3. Pretend you are a leaf falling slowly from a tree.
4. Pretend you are a melting snowman.
5. Maybe some of you have learned how to do the forward roll
   in your school physical education class. If not, here is how
   you do it: find a soft place, place the hands down flat with
   fingers forward, stoop down by bending the knees, pull your
   head in so that your chin is close to your chest, push forward
   with the feet and lower your head, push off so that you land
   on your back and not on your head, and come up to your
   feet.

Remember that all of the helping skills are very important.
Some times boys and girls do not do well in some sports activities. Many times the reason they do not do well is that they
have not taken the time to practice the important helping
skills.

Chapter 3

SKILLS TO MOVE AND
RECEIVE A BALL

IN any kind of game where a ball is used, players must learn how to move the ball and how to receive it. These skills are sometimes called *propelling* skills and *retrieving* skills. This means that a certain game may require you to propel or move a ball in a certain way. Also, certain games will require you to retrieve a ball in a certain way. The skills that we will discuss for moving a ball are *throwing, striking,* and *kicking.* The skills that we will discuss for receiving a ball are *catching* and *trapping.*

THROWING

Throwing simply means that the ball is let go with one or both hands. In general, there are three things needed for success in throwing: (1) the accuracy or direction of the throw, (2) the distance a ball must be thrown, and (3) the amount of force needed to throw the ball.

Whenever anything is let go from one or both hands it could be thought of as an act of throwing. When we think of it in this way, even a child of six months of age is able to do the act of throwing from a sitting position. By four years of age about one out of every five children shows at least some ability in throwing. Between the ages of five and six, over three out of four children have some ability to throw as we have defined it here.

At the early ages boys may throw better than girls. At all ages, boys seem to be generally better than girls in throwing for distance. Although there is not so much difference in throwing for accuracy, boys do tend to throw better. We do not mean that *all* boys will be able to throw better than *all* girls. There are girls who will be able to throw as well or better than boys.

We think of throwing in the form of three *patterns:* (1) the

20

underarm throwing pattern, (2) the sidearm throwing pattern, and (3) the overarm throwing pattern. Even though the ball is let go by one hand or both hands we still use the word *arm* when we think of throwing patterns. The reason for this is that the patterns are thought of as swinging the arm. Sometimes they are called arm-swing patterns.

Underarm Throwing Pattern

In the beginning the very young child starts the underarm throwing pattern by letting the ball go from both hands. Before

Figure 6. UNDERARM THROW!

long, children let go of the ball with one hand, that is, if the ball is small enough to grip with the fingers.

At the start of the throw, the thrower faces in the direction of the throw. The feet are opposite each other and slightly apart. The right arm is in a position nearly up and down with the ground. (Before we go on we should say that this is a discussion about a right-handed thrower. If you are left-handed, you do everything just the opposite of the way it is described here.) To start the throw, the right arm is brought back to a position where it is about parallel with the ground. This is called the backswing. At the same time there is a slight movement of the body to the right. The weight is transferred to the right foot. In the frontswing, when the arm comes forward a step is taken with the left foot. You should always remember that in any throwing pattern you step out with the foot opposite the throwing hand, that is, the foot that is on the other side of the throwing hand. The ball is let go on the frontswing when the arm is about parallel with the ground. During the arm swing the arm is straight: the elbow does not bend. The thrower tries to make about a half a circle with the arm from the backswing to the frontswing. The right foot is carried forward as a part of the follow-through after the ball is let go. Here are the movements again: step forward with the left foot; at the same time swing the arm to the backswing; bring the arm forward and let go of the ball at the end of the frontswing; bring the right foot forward beyond the left foot to follow-through.

The underarm throwing pattern is used in games to pass a ball from one person to another over a short distance. It is also used for pitching in the game of softball.

Sidearm Throwing Pattern

The sidearm throwing action is much like the underarm throwing pattern — the two main differences are the direction the thrower faces and the position of the arm. The thrower faces at a right angle to the direction of the throw: a right-handed thrower has the left side of the body facing in the direction of the throw. The arm is brought to the backswing in a position parallel to the ground. The shift of weight is the same as in the underarm throwing pattern. The arm stays straight, and, again, the thrower tries to make about a half a circle with the arm from the backswing to the frontswing. The sidearm throwing pattern can be used to propel a ball that is too large to grip with one hand. On the backswing, the other hand is used to help control the ball. You can get greater distance with the sidearm throwing pattern, but accuracy may not be as good. An example of the use of this kind of throw is when the ball is thrown in from out-of-bounds in the game of soccer.

Overarm Throwing Pattern

The basic movements of the overarm throwing pattern are about the same as the underarm and sidearm patterns. The

Figure 7. OVERARM THROW!

direction the thrower faces will not always be the same. It will be somewhere between the direction faced in the underarm and sidearm patterns. One big difference in the overarm pattern is in the position of the arm. Remember that in the underarm and sidearm patterns the arm was kept straight. In the overarm pattern the elbow is bent. On the backswing the arm is brought back with the elbow bent and with the arm at a right angle away from the body. The arm is then brought forward, and the ball is let go with a "whiplike" motion. Foot and arm follow-through is the same as in the underarm and sidearm throwing patterns. This pattern is used for throwing a ball that can be gripped with the fingers when accuracy and distance are important, for example, throwing a softball in from the outfield.

STRIKING

Striking means that the ball is caused to move by hitting it. This movement can be caused by a part of the body such as the hand in the game of handball. Most often it will be done with a bat or raquet. The ball can be struck when it is still — batting from a batting tee — or when it is moving — batting in the game of softball. As far as the basic idea is concerned, the movements for striking are about the same as the movements for throwing. The same movements are used; but in order to propel a ball by striking, greater speed is needed. For example, greater speed of movement is needed in the underarm striking pattern when serving a volleyball than in letting a ball go with a short toss in the underarm throw.

KICKING

So far we have talked about moving a ball with the arm and hand. In kicking, the ball is moved with either foot. As early as age two, many children are able to balance on one foot and kick a ball with the other foot. At this early age the child will not have strong action with the kicking leg, and there will be little or no follow-through. As children get older they are able to balance better. Also, they have greater strength in the leg to kick. Usually by age six a child can make a full leg backswing and body lean into the kick with a ball that is not moving.

In kicking, contact can be made with the ball in three ways: (1) with the inside of the foot, (2) with the outside of the foot, and (3) with the instep of the foot. The instep of the foot is that part of the top of the foot from the toes to the ankle. With the exception of these positions of the foot, the basic ideas of kicking are about the same. The kicking leg is swung back, and the knee is bent. The leg swings forward with the foot making

Figure 8. STATIONARY KICK!

contact with the ball. As in the skill of striking, contact with the ball can be made when the ball is either still or moving.

Everyone does not agree on what is the easiest way to kick and what is the hardest way. Our long experience with kicking skills of boys and girls leads us to believe that the following order is a good one. Following are four different ways to kick and we have put them in the order from the easiest to the most difficult.

STATIONARY. Both the ball and the kicker are still or stationary. The kicker simply stands beside the ball and kicks it. The kicker is concerned only with the leg movement and will be more likely to keep the head down and the eyes on the ball.

STATIONARY AND RUN. The ball is in a stationary position, and the kicker takes a short run up to the ball before kicking it. This is more difficult because the kicker must time the run so as to make proper contact with the ball.

KICK FROM HANDS. This is a way of kicking called *punting,* as in football and soccer. The ball is dropped from the hands of the kicker. The kicker takes two or three steps and kicks the ball as it drops. The kicker is kicking a moving ball, but at the same time he has control over the movement before kicking it.

KICKING MOVING BALL. The ball is caused to move by someone other than the kicker. This might be a ball rolled in from a pitcher in a game like kickball. It could also mean kicking a moving ball in a game like soccer. This is probably the most difficult kick. The reason it is so difficult is that the kicker must kick a moving ball, and he has no control over its movement.

CATCHING

Catching is the most common way of retrieving a ball. The catcher gains control of the ball when it is moving in the air or moving along the ground.

One of the child's first experiences with catching is at a very early age. The child sits on the floor with the legs spread, and another person rolls the ball to him. By four years of age, about one out of three children can catch a ball in the air thrown from a very short distance. About half of the children can do this by five years of age, and two out of three children can do this by six years of age.

There are certain basic things to consider in the skill of catching. It is of great importance that the catcher take a position as much "in line" with the ball as possible. In this position it is easier to gain control of the ball. Another important thing is the position of the hands. Usually a ball will come in to the catcher (1) at the waist, (2) above the waist, or (3) below the waist. When the ball comes in at about the waist level, the palms of the hands should be facing each other and the fingers pointing straight ahead. The "heels" of the hands should be close together, depending on the size of the ball: the hands

Figure 9. CATCHING BELOW THE WAIST!

Figure 10. CATCHING ABOVE THE WAIST!

should be closer together for a small ball and farther apart for a large ball. When the ball comes in above the waist the palms face the ball. The fingers point upward with the thumbs as close together as necessary. When the ball comes in below the waist the palms still face the ball, but the fingers point downward. The little fingers are as close together as seems necessary. Again this will depend on the size of the ball. When the ball reaches the hands it is brought in close to the body: the catcher "gives" with the catch. This giving with the catch helps control the ball and absorb the shock. The position of the feet in catching will usually depend upon the speed of the ball when it comes in. Most of the time one foot should be ahead of the other This distance will depend on the speed of the ball.

Very experienced and highly skilled athletes are not always required to keep their eyes on the ball when catching it. You have probably seen an outfielder in baseball turn his back and run for a fly ball. If he is very good he will turn around at just the right time to catch the ball. He has not kept his eyes on the ball all the time it is in the air. Most everyone agrees that boys and girls should keep their eyes on the ball until it is caught. If the eyes are taken off the ball it may be very difficult to catch.

Trapping

Trapping really means that the ball is "caught" with the foot. Since trapping is used mainly in the game of soccer we will discuss the different ways of trapping a ball in our chapter on soccer.

Chapter 4

BASKETBALL

SOMETIMES people wonder how certain games got their start and how they got their name. Many games that we play today began in other countries. Basketball is one of the few games that got its start right here in the United States.

The game was invented by Doctor James Naismith in Springfield, Massachusetts in 1891. The teacher of one of his classes had suggested as an assignment the invention of a game that could be played indoors with a small number of players. Doctor Naismith invented the game of basketball for the class assignment, and also so that there would be a game that could be used to fill in time between the end of football season in the fall and the start of baseball in the spring.

In the beginning, the game of basketball was much different than it is today. There were nine players on each team. They were allowed to throw, bat, or pass the ball. The first game was played with peach baskets; this is how it got the name of basketball. In the early days the number of players sometimes depended on how much space there was for playing. After a while, the rules changed so that there were five on a men's team and six on a women's team. In the beginning, the game was played only by grown men and women. Today it is played by children as well as adults, although the rules may be simpler for boys and girls than they are for men and women.

Interest in the game of basketball has spread so much that it is now played in many countries around the world. It has become a very important part of the Olympic Games, which are held every four years. People of all ages seem to enjoy trying to put a ball through a basket.

Basketball as played today can take place on a court as small as 42 feet by 72 feet. The largest size is 50 feet by 90 feet. The basketball goals at either end of the court are 10 feet high with each team having its own goal. Sometimes for boys and girls the goals may be 8 or 9 feet. This shorter distance can make it easier for them to get the ball into the basket. The regular size of the ball is 29 1/2 inches around. Smaller balls of 29 inches around are used by players under high school age. Even much smaller balls can be used because they are easier for younger players to handle.

The purpose of the game is for one team to score more points than the other team. A goal counts two points, and a free throw (caused when certain rules are broken) counts one point. The game requires many different kinds of skills. These skills include *passing, catching, shooting, dribbling, pivoting* and *guarding*.

PASSING

Passing simply means that the ball is transferred from one player to another. There are many different kinds of passes. Each one has its own purpose. The kind of pass used will depend on two things. The first thing is the distance the ball has to travel. Second, the position in which the ball is caught may cause the player to choose the kind of pass to make. The following are some of the more widely used passes.

Chest Pass

This pass is probably the one most often used in basketball. It is good to use when the ball is to be passed a short distance. The ball is held chest high. The fingers grip the ball and are spread lightly over the center of the ball. The thumbs are close together. The elbows are bent and close to the body. In the passing action the arms go forward from the shoulders and the elbows straighten. The ball is let go with a snap of the wrists. The ball can be passed a greater distance if the knees are bent and a short step is taken with one foot.

Bounce Pass

This pass can be done with one or both hands. It is probably

Figure 11. CHEST PASS!

better to use both hands as this makes it easier to control the ball. In this pass, a bounce is used so that the ball can bounce into the other player's hands. When two hands are used, it is done about the same way as the chest pass. The difference is that the ball is passed low to hit the floor rather than chest high. This is not an easy pass to make, and it takes lots of practice. The passer must judge the place on the floor to bounce the ball. It is a good idea to make the ball hit the floor about three-fourths of the distance from the passer to the catcher. This kind of pass will cause the ball to be caught at about the waist. Some beginners make the mistake of bouncing the ball straight downward rather than pushing it forward. The good thing about the bounce pass is that it sometimes allows the passer to get the ball to the catcher before it can be blocked.

Figure 12. BOUNCE PASS!

One-handed Underarm Pass

This pass is done with the underarm throwing pattern explained in Chapter 3. Because the ball is too big to be gripped, the other hand is put on top of the ball. This will keep the ball from falling out of the throwing hand. The other hand is taken away when the ball is brought forward. This pass is good to use for short distances to get the ball quickly to another player.

Shoulder Pass

This pass is sometimes called the *baseball pass* or the *one-hand overarm pass*. It is done with the overarm throwing pattern explained in Chapter 3. This pass is not used too often by young players because it is hard to control. It is useful when passing a distance. If a teammate breaks away and gets down the floor it can be a good pass to get the ball there quickly. It should be remembered that as a general rule short passes are better than longer ones. It should also be remembered that the longer the pass the better chance it has to be caught by a member of the other team.

Figure 13. SHOULDER PASS!

The shoulder pass is begun with one foot just ahead of the other. The hand that is not used to throw the ball is used to steady it. This helps the passer to keep from losing control of the ball. The ball is brought forward above the shoulder and past the ear. When the ball is let go there should be a snap of the wrist the same as in the chest pass.

Figure 14. TWO-HANDED OVERHEAD PASS!

Two-handed Overhead Pass

The ball is held over the head with both hands. It is about one foot in front of the head. The fingers are spread above the center of the ball, and the elbows are slightly bent. The passer steps forward with one foot and passes the ball forward at the same time. At the end of the pass the arms and fingers will be pointing upward. This is a good pass to use when the distance is longer than is needed for the chest pass.

CATCHING

You will probably remember that we talked about the general things concerned with catching in Chapter 3. Some of those things will be said again because of the way they apply to basketball. An important thing in catching in the game of basketball is that the catcher should move to meet the ball. This movement is sometimes called *cutting* and will shorten the distance the ball has to travel. Also, it will help to shut off a player of the other team who tries to block the ball. When the ball is caught it should be brought in as close to the body as possible. This will help to keep the person who is guarding the passer from getting the ball.

We have already said how the hands should be held when a ball is caught at the waist, above the waist, or below the waist. Usually a basketball is caught in the last two positions, above or below the waist. When catching a basketball above the waist keep your eyes on the ball. The hands are forward toward the ball with the fingers pointing up. The knees are slightly bent; the feet are apart; and the body leans slightly forward. When the ball is caught the fingers are spread, and the hands and arms give with the ball. This helps to slow down the force of the ball and makes it easier to control. Remember to bring the ball in close to the body.

In catching the basketball below the waist, again, the eyes are kept on the ball. The fingers point downward and are well spread and the hands and arms give with the ball when it is caught. Try not to shift the hands on the ball — you might want to pass it quickly with the same motion.

SHOOTING

All of the skills of basketball are important. Because putting the ball through the hoop is the method of scoring, shooting is one of the most important skills.

We have already said that the regular height of the goal is 10 feet from the floor. Most people think it is best to have the goal at 8 or 9 feet for boys and girls who are 12 years of age or younger. The reason is that they have a much better chance of getting the ball in the basket.

The basic patterns of basket shooting are those of throwing, which we talked about in Chapter 3. Depending on the height of the basket, three things need to be remembered. First, allowance must be made for the angle when the ball is let go. The second thing is how much force is needed to send the ball to the basket. The third important thing to remember is that the eyes should be kept on the rim of the goal.

There are about five different kinds of shots in the game of basketball:

1. Two-handed Underhand Shot
2. Two-handed Chest Shot
3. One-handed Push Shot
4. Lay-up Shot
5. Jump Shot

Two-handed Underhand Shot

This is probably the easiest way for boys and girls to shoot. It is best used as a free throw shot. If used as a shot while the ball is in play, it is easy to block. The ball is held about waist high. The fingers of both hands are under the ball with the thumbs pointing upward. The knees are bent and the ball brought downward between the legs. The ball is then brought upward, and the knees become straight. The ball is let go when the arms are straight toward the basket.

We have said that this is a good way to shoot free throws.

Figure 15. TWO-HANDED UNDERHAND SHOT!

However, most players of high school age and older use other kinds of shots for free throws. One big exception is Rick Barry, the basketball star of the Houston Rockets. He uses the two-handed underhand shot for free throws. The fact that he is one

Figure 16. TWO-HANDED CHEST SHOT!

of the best "foul shooters" in all of basketball is reason enough for believing that it is a good way to shoot free throws.

Two-handed Chest Shot

This shot is a good one for beginners because the ball is easy to control. The two-handed chest shot is like the chest pass, but the angle where the ball is let go is different. The ball is held in both hands about chest high. The ball is tipped back on the fingers, which are spread and above the center of the ball. The ball is then pushed toward the goal. The shooter tries to get a proper arch on the flight of the ball. Either foot can be ahead of the other, or the feet can be together. The knees should be bent. When the ball is let go the legs are straightened. At the end of the shot, the arms are stretched, and the fingers point upward toward the basket.

One-handed Push Shot

The ball is balanced by the fingers of the shooting hand. The other hand supports the ball from underneath. One foot is slightly ahead of the other. The knees are bent slightly. The feet are spread at a distance where the shooter feels comfortable. Most of the weight is on the front foot. The hand underneath the ball is taken away as the ball is pushed toward the basket. When the ball is let go, the fingers of the shooting hand point toward the basket. The arm is stretched to full length upward. This shot may not be easy because it is harder to control the ball with one hand than it is with two. However, if the shooter can control the ball, this shot is hard to guard against. The reason for its being hard to guard against is that the shot starts high and the shooter can let go of the ball quickly.

Lay-up Shot

This shot is a little bit like the one-handed push shot. The ball is aimed at the backboard when the shooter is close in under the basket. The reason for this aim is that the ball is banked against the backboard into the basket; that is, the

Figure 17. ONE-HANDED PUSH SHOT!

shooter "lays" the ball on the backboard. The right-handed shooter takes off close to the basket from the left foot and jumps as high as possible toward the goal. For the left-handed

Figure 18. LAY-UP SHOT!

Figure 19. JUMP SHOT!

shooter the takeoff is with the right foot. The player usually comes to the basket from the side with a bounce of the ball, or he may catch a pass from a teammate as he runs in. It is probably a good idea to practice the shot first without the jump. This will give the shooter an idea of where the ball should hit the backboard so that it will drop into the basket.

Jump Shot

The jump shot uses the same movement as the one-handed push shot. The shot is made after jumping into the air from the floor with both feet. The jump shot is hard to guard against because the ball is higher when the shooter lets go. At the same

Figure 20. DRIBBLING!

time it is a difficult shot to make and takes a great deal of practice.

DRIBBLING

Dribbling means that the player controls the ball by bouncing it several times. The fingers are well spread so that it will be easier to control the ball. The knees are bent to keep the body low. The body leans forward; the ball is held just a little higher than the knees. The beginning dribbler will probably need to keep the eyes on the ball. After the skill is learned, the player should practice keeping the head up. The first bounce is started by laying the ball well out in front and pushing with the dribbling hand. Remember that the ball is pushed toward the floor and not slapped downward.

PIVOTING

The basic skill of pivoting was described in Chapter 2. In basketball, pivoting is used to change direction when the player is standing in place. It takes place when a player who is holding the ball steps once, or more than once, in any direction with the same foot. The other foot is the pivot foot and stays in contact with the floor. The weight of the body is equally placed on both feet. The ball is held firmly with the fingertips of both hands. The elbows point outward to help protect the ball from a player on the other team. The player can turn in any direction on the pivot foot. Remember not to drag the pivot foot because this movement is the same as walking with the ball.

GUARDING

Up until now we have talked about skills with the ball. The skill of guarding is used to try to keep a member of the other team from shooting, passing or dribbling. An important rule in guarding is that you should try to keep between the basket and the person you are guarding. In guarding, the feet are spread, the knees are bent. The arms are outstretched to the sides. One arm can be up and the other arm down. In this position you are ready to move in any direction. That movement is usually

Figure 21. GUARDING!

done with the skill of sliding, which was described in Chapter 1. When the person you are guarding gets the ball you should try to get about two or three feet away from him. In your guarding position you are ready not only to block a pass or a shot, but also to stop a dribble.

REBOUNDING

Whenever a shot does not go into the basket it will probably rebound back to the playing area, that is, if it does not go out of bounds. Rebounding is a skill used to try to get the ball after it has bounced off the backboard or the basket. This is one of the most difficult skills to learn. The reason it is so difficult is that the player must time the jump and rebound of the ball. A player who is able to time these two movements well will be in the right spot to get the ball. The player jumps from the floor and stretches the arms toward the basket. If the ball is caught it should be brought in close to the body. When the player has the ball and the feet are on the floor, he should bend forward to protect the ball. If a person is successful in rebounding at his own basket his team will still control the ball. Getting a rebound at the other team's basket means that a player will have taken the ball so that the other team cannot shoot again right away. Although it helps to be tall in rebounding, being able to jump high and time the jump are also very important.

TEAM PLAY

The most important thing in basketball is team play. This means *offensive* team play when your team has the ball and *defensive* team play when the other team has the ball. The following are some important things to remember about offensive team play:

1. Players should try to be aware at all times where their teammates are on the floor.
2. Players should be thinking about getting into an empty space to get away from their guard.
3. When a player passes the ball he should keep moving and not stand around.
4. Players will usually have more success with short passes than with long ones.
5. When shooting, make sure that you have a good chance of making the basket, otherwise, you should pass to another player.

6. When you have the ball there are only three things you can do. You can pass, shoot, or dribble. You must decide quickly what is the best thing to do. If you do not have a good shot it is a good idea to pass the ball. Dribbling should probably be used only when, for some reason, you are not able to pass the ball.

The following are some important things to remember about defensive team play:

1. Most guarding is done in the other team's offensive area of the floor. Usually there is little need to guard all over the floor. An exception would be late in a game when your team is behind in the scoring; in that situation it might be wise to guard all over the floor.
2. A player should always know who he is supposed to guard.
3. When guarding, try never to cross the feet. Use the skill of sliding instead.
4. It may be a good idea to have one person stay back to guard near the other team's basket.
5. In guarding, always keep between the basket and the player you are guarding.

GAMES TO PRACTICE BASKETBALL SKILLS

Most all of the skills we have talked about can be practiced by one person alone. However, with some of them it is better to have a partner. Better still, if there are several people, you can play games to practice the skill. Everyone knows it is more fun to play games than it is to practice the skills. We do not mean that you should not practice the skills by yourself. Many basketball players spend long hours practicing on their own.

There are all kinds of games in which you can practice basketball skills. The ones that we are explaining here are just a few examples. Many times you and your friends can make up games of your own that are good for practicing certain basketball skills. The following games use one or more of the skills of passing, catching, dribbling, shooting, and guarding. They do not need to be played on a regular basketball court.

Bear in the Circle

Two circles are formed: each circle is a team and can have

four or more players. A member of the other team, the bear, stands in the center of each circle. The players in the circle pass the ball around, and the bear tries to touch it. If the bear touches the ball, a point is scored for that team. To begin with, you should decide how long you will play the game. At the end of that time the team with the highest score is the winner. Everyone on both teams should have a turn at being the bear.

Keep Away

There can be as many teams as you want in this game: there can be four or more players on a team. It is better to have more teams so that there are not many players on a team; this way more players will get a chance to handle the ball. Play starts with one of the teams having the ball. This team passes the ball around to its own players. Players of all the other teams try to get the ball. If a member of one of the teams gets the ball, that team starts play again with the ball. All of the rules of basketball are used, and the idea of the game is to see which team can keep the ball for the longest amount of time.

Tag Ball

This game is like *Keep Away* except that one member on each of the teams is picked to be *It*. The purpose of the game is to tag the person on a team who is It with the ball. When this happens the tagging team scores a point. All of the rules of basketball are used. The ball can be advanced to It by passing or dribbling. All players who are It should stand out in some way, perhaps with an armband, so that the others can tell easily which players are It.

Half-court Basketball

All the rules of basketball are used. The only difference from the regular game is that only one-half of the court is used: both teams use the same goal. When a goal is made or the other team gets the ball, the other team must start again with the ball. Play usually begins again somewhere around the free throw line or in the center of the court. This is a good game if you or one of your friends have a basketball goal in your yard or in your driveway.

Chapter 5

SOCCER

THE game of soccer is different than most other games. Soccer is played mainly with the feet, while just about all other games are played by using the hands to control the ball.

When the game of soccer was first started it was not called by that name. To begin with, it was called *Association Football*. The rules for this game were made in the year 1863 by the *London Football Association*. Later the word "Association" was shortened to "Assoc," which was later changed to "Soccer," which is what the game is called today. In the last few years soccer has become very popular and is played all over the world. It probably has its greatest popularity in certain South American countries. However, in more recent years it has become very popular in the United States. This popularity is particularly true of the game as played by boys and girls. Just a few years ago not many boys and girls in this country had heard of soccer, now it is played by thousands.

The game of soccer is played on a field 130 yards by 100 yards. This is the largest the field can be. The smallest the field is supposed to be is 100 yards by 50 yards. There is a goal at each end of the field. These goals are made up of two posts, which are 8 yards apart and a crossbar on the posts, which is 8 feet above the ground. The game is played with a round heavy ball, which is about 27 to 28 inches around.

The idea of the game is for one team to score more goals than the other team. To score a goal a player must get the ball through the goal and under the crossbar. This must be done with the feet or head. There are eleven players on each of two teams. They move the ball by kicking it with their feet or hitting it with their heads. There is very little use of the hands. However, the hands can be used by the goalkeeper. Also, when the ball goes out-of-bounds it can be thrown in with the hands.

The game is often changed for boys and girls your age. Many

times a smaller playing area is used. Also, a much lighter ball can be used, and sometimes the rules allow for more use of the hands.

WAYS TO MOVE THE BALL

We have already said that soccer is a game played mainly

Figure 22. KICKING WITH THE INSTEP!

with the feet. For this reason, kicking is one of the ways that is used most to move the ball. There are two other ways that the ball can be moved. These are with the head, which is called "heading," and with the hands to "throw in" from out-of-bounds.

Kicking

There are about six different kinds of kicks that are used in soccer: (1) kicking with the instep, (2) kicking with the inside of the foot, (3) kicking with the outside of the foot, (4) punting, (5) volley kick, and (6) foot dribbling.

Kicking with the Instep

Kicking with the instep of the foot is the kind of kick that is probably the most used in soccer. It can be used for passing the ball to a teammate and for shooting at the goal. The foot *not* used for kicking is even with the ball. The kicking leg is back, and the body leans forward a little. The ankle is downward so that the instep meets the ball. Remember that the instep is that part of the foot just in back of the toes on the top of the foot.

Kicking with the Inside of the Foot

The inside edge of the foot meets the ball. The toe of the kicking foot is turned out. The leg is bent a little at the knee. When the inside of the foot meets the ball, the leg swings across in front of the body. Just as the foot meets the ball in front of the body, the knee is straightened. The foot should meet the ball just below the center. Usually the kicker takes a short run up to the ball while it is on the ground and not moving. In kicking the ball with the inside of the foot, the ball can be kicked a long way. This kind of kick can also be used to make a short pass to a teammate or to try to kick for a goal.

Kicking with the Outside of the Foot

This kick is used mainly for short distances to get the ball to

Figure 23. KICKING WITH THE INSIDE OF THE FOOT!

a teammate. It can also be used to get the ball away from a player who is running toward you. The foot that is *not* being used to kick is about 6 or 8 inches behind the ball and to the side of it. The knee of the kicking leg is bent. The kicking leg swings across in front of the other leg. The outside of the foot meets the ball as the kicking foot swings past the other leg.

Figure 24. KICKING WITH THE OUTSIDE OF THE FOOT!

Punting

This is the kick that we call "kick from hands" in Chapter 3. The goalkeeper is the only player allowed to punt the ball. The punt is used to clear the ball over the heads of the other players down the field.

Punting is a little bit like kicking with the instep. The difference is that the ball is held out in front and dropped as it is kicked. If you are the goalkeeper (goalie) and are going to punt with the right foot, the ball is held out in front of the right leg. The ball is held a little above the waist. You take a step on the left foot, and the right leg is brought back. When you drop the ball you swing the right leg forward and upward. Your foot hits the ball with the instep of the foot.

Figure 25. VOLLEY KICK!

Volley Kick

The volley is a kick that is made while the ball is in the air. Because it is very hard to kick the ball while it is in the air, the volley kick is not always allowed in soccer games played by boys and girls. When it is used, the following is one way to do it: the player stands with the kicking foot in back of the other foot; he faces the ball as it comes in and leans forward slightly; when the ball gets to the player, the leg of the kicking foot is raised, and the weight is shifted to the other foot; the knee is bent just a little, and the toes point downward; the foot meets the ball at the top of the instep, and the foot goes forward and upward.

There is a good way to practice the volley kick. Have a friend stand a short distance away from you and toss the ball toward you. He should not stand too close because he could get hit with the ball.

Dribbling

Dribbling is a way of controlling the ball with the feet when

Figure 26. DRIBBLING!

you are moving along. It is a very light kick: the foot just touches the ball and moves it along.

To begin the dribble, the weight of the body is equal on both feet. The ball should be kept about 10 to 12 inches in front of the dribbler. The arms can be out to the side to help you keep

Figure 27. HEADING!

your balance. The head should be over the ball. The ball is tapped easily with either foot. You dribble first with one foot and then the other. You can use the inside or the outside of the foot, but it is easier to dribble with the inside of the foot. When you first try to dribble, do it very slowly. Remember that the ball should be only about 10 or 12 inches in front of you.

Heading

Heading the soccer ball means that it is hit with the front or side of the forehead. Sometimes heading is not allowed in soccer games played by boys and girls. The main reason it is not allowed is that sometimes young players do not do it well, and they might hurt themselves. If it is used, we think that it should be done with a ball that is much lighter and softer than a regular soccer ball.

As the ball comes toward the player, the head is dropped back. The arms are raised. The weight is shifted to the back foot. The next move is to bring the body forward and upward. At this time the head meets the ball. The ball is met with the side or front of the forehead. At the end of the movement you land on both feet; the ankles and knees are bent; and the arms are out to the sides for balance.

The Throw In

Whenever the ball goes out-of-bounds over the sidelines it has to be put in play again. It is put in play with the *throw in* as the player stands out-of-bounds. The throw in must be done from behind the head with both hands. Part of both feet must be on the ground until the player lets the ball go.

The throw in for soccer is very much like the two-handed overhead pass in basketball. You begin the throw with one foot ahead of the other. The ball is held above the head with both hands. As you throw the ball in, you shift your weight to the front leg. Try to snap your wrists so as to get more force behind the ball.

WAYS TO STOP THE BALL

The way to stop the ball in soccer is called *trapping*. There are many kinds of traps, including (1) body traps, (2) foot traps, and (3) leg traps.

Body Traps

Body traps are a way to stop the ball with the body. It is done in a way so that the ball will drop to the ground at a place where the player can quickly dribble or kick it. The body trap is used when the ball is coming from a high volley, or when a player does not want a high ball to get past him.

The body is straight; the weight is on both feet; and the eyes

Figure 28. BODY TRAP!

are kept on the ball. As the ball comes in waist high or above, the body is moved backward. The weight is now on the heels, and the arms can be out to the side for balance. Just as the ball meets the body, the player should "give" with it. At the same time the player takes a little jump backward. The player tries to make a "pocket" for the ball as it hits his chest. When girls use the body trap it is a good idea for them to fold their arms over their chest. This way the ball will hit their folded arms. If the body trap is done in the right way the ball will roll down the front of the player. He should then be ready to dribble or kick.

Figure 29. TRAP WITH SOLE OF FOOT!

Foot Traps

Foot traps are used to stop a ball that is rolling or bouncing along the ground. The two ways to trap the ball with the foot are (1) with the sole of the foot and (2) with the side of the foot.

Trapping with the Sole of the Foot

The player first needs to line himself up with the ball so that it is coming straight at him. When the ball reaches the player, he raises the foot he is going to use to trap the ball. This foot is about 8 inches from the ground with the toes pointing upward. He quickly brings the sole of the foot down on the ball. The ball is trapped between the ground and the sole of the foot. It is best to use this trap when the ball is moving slowly. Remember to keep your eyes on the ball.

Trapping with the Side of the Foot

This trap is done pretty much the same way as the trap with the sole of the foot. The big difference is in the way the ball comes to you. It is better to use the side of the foot if the ball is bouncing from the side. Also, it might be better to use this trap when the ball is coming in fairly fast. You place your weight on the foot that is *not* going to trap the ball. You turn the foot that is to trap the ball outward so that the ball meets the inside of the foot. As soon as the ball touches the foot you should allow the foot to give with the ball. With practice you should be able to make the ball stop where you want it to stop. If the ball bounces forward off your foot it means that you did not allow the foot to give enough with the ball.

Leg Traps

There are two ways of trapping the ball with the legs: (1) with one leg (or the single leg trap) and (2) with both legs (or the double leg trap).

Figure 30. TRAP WITH SIDE OF FOOT!

Single Leg Trap

In the single leg trap, the player tries to get in line with the ball. The foot of the leg doing the trapping is placed a little in back of the other foot. Just the toes of this foot touch the ground. The knees of both legs are bent. If you are trapping with the right leg you should turn just a little to your left. When the ball meets the leg, the lower part of the leg, or shin, presses against the ball and traps it. If you do it in the right way, the ball should be in place in front of you where you can kick it or dribble it.

Figure 31. SINGLE LEG TRAP!

Double Leg Trap

When you use the double leg trap your feet should be slightly apart with the toes pointing outward. The knees are bent a little more than in the single leg trap. The reason for this position is that you try to trap the ball against the ground with both shins. After you trap the ball you should raise the body up straight. The ball will be right in front of you where you can dribble it or kick it. It is a good idea to put your arms out to the side. They will help you balance yourself and will keep you from falling.

Figure 32. DOUBLE LEG TRAP!

TACKLING

When we use the word "tackling" you probably think of football. In soccer, tackling means that you try to take the ball away from a player on the other team. We call this tackling the ball. When you are good at tackling you can cause another player to make a poor kick or to overrun the ball. That is the purpose of tackling the ball in soccer. The two ways of tackling the ball are (1) the straight tackle and (2) the hook tackle.

Straight Tackle

In the straight tackle you try to get in front of a player who is dribbling. You should try to put your foot on the ball. This movement is a little bit like trapping the ball with the sole of the foot. If you can get your foot on the ball you should try to kick it or hold it until the dribbler overruns the ball.

Hook Tackle

In the hook tackle you also try to get in front of a player who is dribbling. You then step quickly to one side. You reach in with one leg and use that leg as a "hook." You try to draw the ball out to the side. You have to bend the other leg so that you can reach in a greater distance with the hooking leg. You must be careful not to run into the player when you are trying to tackle the ball.

TEAM PLAY

Just as in the game of basketball, team play is very important in the game of soccer. This means *offensive* team play when your team has the ball and *defensive* team play when the other team has the ball. The following are some important things to remember about offensive team play:

1. When possible try to use short kicks. It is easier for the other team to get the ball when you use long kicks.
2. Try to make sure that you have the ball under control before you try to kick it.
3. When kicking it to a teammate, try to kick the ball ahead of him.
4. Know where your place is on the field and try to stay pretty much in that place.

The following are some important things to remember in defensive team play:

1. Get ready to tackle the ball as soon as a member of the other team gets it.
2. Always be thinking about the kind of trap you are going to use on the ball.
3. When you get control of the ball from a member of the other team, get it to one of your own teammates as soon as possible.

GAMES TO PRACTICE SOCCER SKILLS

Most all of the soccer skills we have explained can be practiced by one person. In some of them it is probably better to have a partner. There are many games you can play to help you with soccer skills. On the following pages we explain how to play some of these games.

Line Soccer

In this game you will be able to practice kicking, dribbling, and trapping. There are two teams with about eight players on a team. You will need a playing area of about 30 feet by 60 feet. The two teams form lines facing each other. The idea of the game is for a player to kick the ball over the other team's goal line.

To start the game, the ball is placed in the center of the playing field. Two players go to the center of the field and put their right foot on the ball. A signal is given, and each of these players tries to kick the ball across the other team's goal line. These two players can run all over the field kicking or dribbling the ball. All of the other players try to keep the ball from going over the goal line. They do this by trapping or kicking the ball. Two points are scored when a player kicks the ball over the other goal line. Only the players in the center are allowed to score. The players should try to keep the ball below the waist of the other players. It is a foul if the ball is touched with the hands or arms. Kicking the ball over the head is also a

oul. The penalty for a foul is a free kick, which is made from
he center of the field. The game is over when everyone has had
ı chance to be one of the two players in the center of the field.

Corner Kickball

Corner Kickball is a good game to practice the skills of drib-
ıling and kicking. There are two teams of about ten players on
ach team. The playing area can be about 40 feet by 75 feet.
The idea of the game is to kick the ball through the other
eam's end zone. The size of the end zone is about 15 feet from
he front line to the back line.

To begin the game the ball is placed in the center of the field.
On a signal, a corner player from each team runs into the
enter and tries to kick or dribble the ball into the other's end
one. The other players stay in the end zone and try to stop the
ball with any part of their body other than their hands and
arms. When a goal is scored, two other players come to the
enter. If a goal is not scored after a certain amount of time,
two new players come to the center of the field to play the ball.
It is a foul if there is tripping, pushing, or touching the ball
with the hands. If there is a foul, the other team gets a free kick
from 15 yards out. The game can be played for about 10 min-
utes or longer if you wish.

Soccer Dodgeball

Kicking and trapping are skills that can be practiced in this
game. There can be eight or ten players on a team. One team
forms a circle. The other team scatters around inside this circle.
The players who make up the circle try to hit the players in the
circle with the ball. They try to hit them by kicking the ball at
them. The players in the circle are not allowed to use their
hands to stop the ball. If one of the players in the center of the
circle is hit with the ball below the waist, he becomes a member
of the outer circle. If the game is played all the way through,
the winner would be the last player in the circle who has not
been hit with the ball.

Circle Trap

Any number of players can be used in this game. All of the players but one form a circle. This one player stands in the center of the circle. One of the players making the circle starts the game by rolling the ball across the circle. The players making the circle try to keep the ball moving by kicking it to one another. The player in the center of the circle tries to trap the ball. If he is able to do it, he changes places with the player who was the last one to kick the ball. If the ball goes out of the circle the one nearest to it goes to the center of the circle. If the player in the center of the circle is not able to trap the ball after a period of time, another player should be chosen to go to the center.

Circle Soccer

A circle is formed with any number of players. The players kick a ball around in the circle as quickly as they can. The idea of the game is to keep the ball from going out of the circle. If the ball goes out of the circle it counts a point against the two players on either side of the ball where it went out of the circle. This means that when the ball goes out of the circle between two players each one has a point scored against him. The ball should be kept on the ground when kicking it. It should not be kicked above the waist. The game can be made more interesting by using two balls at the same time.

Hit Pin Soccer

Two teams of six to eight players each form lines about 15 feet apart. Several objects, such as milk cartons or cans, are placed in the middle between the two teams. The players of each team kick the ball back and forth trying to knock over the objects. A point is scored when an object is knocked over. At the end of a certain amount of time, the team with the highest score is the winner.

Square Soccer

Any number of players can be used in this game. The number of players is divided into four teams. Each team stands in line side by side. All four teams make a square. The players face inward. All of the players of each team have a number, that is, if there are six players on a team one player is number one, another is number two, and so on. A leader is chosen, and he drops the ball in the center of the square. At the same time the leader calls a number. All four of the players with this number run to the center and try to get the ball through any side of the square. The players at the side of the square are goalkeepers. They can use their hands to stop the ball. As soon as a score is made by getting the ball through any side of the square, another number is called. The member of the team who got the ball through the side of the square scores a point for this team. The game can be played for a certain amount of time or until every player's number is called. Square Soccer is a good game to help you practice kicking, trapping, and goal tending.

These are just a few ideas, and you and your friends can probably make up many games of your own to practice soccer skills.

Chapter 6

SOFTBALL

SOFTBALL is a form of baseball, but it is different in the following ways:

1. The game can be played indoors as well as outdoors.
2. A ball larger and softer is used rather than the hard baseball.
3. The distance between the bases in softball is 55 feet, while in baseball this distance is 90 feet.
4. The pitching distance is 43 feet for men and 35 feet for women. The pitching distance for baseball is 60 1/2 feet.
5. Pitching in softball is done with the underarm throwing pattern. The overarm throwing pattern is allowed in all other parts of the game.

Softball was started in the early 1900s by American professional baseball players. They played softball to keep in practice during the offseason. At that time the game was called *Indoor Baseball*. It was a good game because it gave professional players a chance to practice during the winter months.

During the late 1920s the game became very popular in Canada. Players from that country began to play the game outdoors on playgrounds and it became known as *Playground Ball*. Sometime later the name of the game was changed to *Softball*, and that is the name that it goes by today.

It was not long before there was a great deal of interest in the game in the United States. This interest actually started about 1930. The game is now played by thousands of men and women and boys and girls all over the country.

The most important skills in softball are throwing, catching, batting, and running. As we have said before, running is a skill used in most all games. In softball it is used to run and field the ball and to run around the bases. The skills of catching, throwing, and batting in softball are not easy to learn. One of the reasons they are not easy is that players use a much smaller

70

ball in softball than they use in many other games. This sometimes makes the ball hard to control. We want to talk about
some of the skills that are important to make you a good softball player.

THROWING

The skills of throwing and the patterns of throwing were
explained in Chapter 3. For this reason, you should look back
into that chapter to read about the different ways of throwing.

Overarm Throw

In softball, the overarm throwing pattern is used almost all
of the time in throwing to bases and returning the ball from the
outfield. Balls thrown to a base and between bases should be
thrown fairly hard. You should try to make the ball travel in a
straight line.

Underarm Throw

In softball, the underarm throwing pattern is used mainly for
pitching. Sometimes it is used as a short toss when a ball is
fielded close to a base, for example, when it is fielded too close
to use the overarm throwing pattern.

CATCHING

Catching in softball is done pretty much the same way as it
was explained in Chapter 3. However, you should remember
that the ball is smaller and might be harder to control. It is a
good idea for you to practice catching balls that are thrown to
you before trying to catch batted balls. It is easier to catch a ball
that is thrown than to catch a ball that is batted. Even though
the game is called softball, the ball is not as "soft" as one
would think. For this reason, a glove is worn so that the shock
of the ball will not be so great. Also, it is easier to catch the ball
with a glove. By using a glove, you really have a larger hand to
catch a smaller ball.

FIELDING

Catching or stopping a ball after it has been hit by a batter is called fielding. When the ball comes to you through the air it is called a *fly ball*. When it comes to you along the ground it is called a *ground ball* or a *grounder*.

Fielding Fly Balls

When we talked about catching before, we said it is important to get lined up with the ball. It is very important in fielding a fly ball because the ball comes in with such force. The fielder should try to keep his eyes on the ball: as soon as the ball leaves the bat he should try to track it with the eyes. Watch the ball closely as it comes through the air and then get ready to catch it. When the ball is high you should try to catch it above the chin. The thumbs are together with the fingers pointing upward. When the ball drops low you should try to catch it near the waist. The little fingers are close together. On either a high ball or a low ball you make a little basket by spreading and cupping the fingers.

The body leans forward with the arms bent. The weight is placed evenly on both feet. If you run up on the ball you shift your weight to the front foot when you catch it. Let your bare hand follow the ball into the glove to hold the ball.

Fielding fly balls is not an easy skill, and sometimes boys and girls make mistakes. Here are some of these mistakes. Be sure you do not make them.

1. Not lining yourself up with the ball.
2. Running up too soon to meet the ball (you may overrun it).
3. Not running up soon enough to meet the ball (it might drop in front of you).
4. Catching the ball in front of the eyes. (When you do this you can drop the ball because you take your eyes off it. Remember that we said to keep your eyes on the ball.)
5. Trying to catch the ball with one hand under it and the other hand over it (remember that the hands should be

Figure 33. FIELDING FLY BALL!

side by side).

6. Not giving with the ball. (If you do not give with it, the ball will probably hit your glove and bounce out.)

Fielding Ground Balls

When you see the ball coming toward you, try your best to

get in line with it. If you are right-handed, your left foot should be forward. Bend your body at the hips, knees, and ankles: try to keep the upper part of the body straight. Point your fingers downward and place the hands just opposite the left foot; you then try to contact the ball just inside the left foot with the left hand. Cover the ball with the right hand so that you get control of it. Keep your eyes on the ball at all times. As soon as you field the ball you are in a position to raise the body for the throw.

Figure 34. FIELDING GROUND BALL!

PITCHING

Pitching in softball is done with the underarm throwing pattern, which was explained in Chapter 3. At the start of the pitch the feet must be parallel. The ball is held with both hands, and the pitcher faces the batter. For a right-handed pitcher, the right arm is swung back. The body turns slightly. The right arm is brought forward, and the ball is let go off the ends of the fingers. The ball should be at about the level of the hip when it is pitched. The right foot is brought up so that the pitcher is in good position to field the ball if it is hit by the batter. The following are some important things for a pitcher

Figure 35. PITCHING!

to remember:

1. Step toward the batter when you let the ball go.
2. Aim at a target.
3. Follow through with your pitching arm.
4. At the end of the pitch, the fingers point toward the target.
5. The target is about three feet above home plate.
6. Work together with the catcher.

BATTING

Batting is a striking skill and was explained in Chapter 3. One of the first things to think about in batting is how to grip the bat. If you are right-handed, the left hand is wrapped around the bat at about two inches from the end. The right hand is wrapped around the bat just above the left hand. If the bat is heavy, or if it is a long bat, you can wrap the left hand around much higher on the bat. This is called the "choke" grip. Swing a bat several times to make sure you are gripping it in a way that feels best.

A right-handed batter stands with the left side of the body facing the pitcher. The feet are parallel and about shoulder-

Figure 36. BATTING!

width apart. The bat is held back of the head. It is about shoulder high. The arms are bent at the elbows and are held away from the body. The batter watches the pitched ball. When it leaves the pitcher's hand, the batter's weight should be shifted to the rear foot. If the batter decides to strike at the ball, he swings the bat forward, level with the ground. The weight is shifted to the left foot. The trade mark (printing on the bat) should be facing the batter.

Bunting

Bunting is a form of batting used to hit a ball a very short distance. Bunting can be done to surprise the fielders. It is usually done by very fast runners. They have to have a lot of speed in order to get to first base before the bunt is fielded.

In bunting, the batter should stand up straight. Your feet are apart so that you can get the bat in front of the ball anywhere in the "strike zone." The left hand stays in the same place on the bat. The right hand slides about halfway up the bat. Do not swing at the ball; just let it hit the bat.

Fungo Batting

Used only in practice, fungo batting is when the batter throws the ball up himself and hits it. For a right-handed batter, the bat is held with the right hand. It can rest on the shoulder, or it can be held out to the side. The ball is held in the left hand. The weight is on the back foot. A step is taken to the side with the left foot. The ball is tossed up high enough to give time to get the left hand on the bat for the swing. You should practice throwing the ball up several times before swinging the bat. This will give you an idea of how high you will need to throw the ball.

BASERUNNING

Before we get into the skill of baserunning, it might be a good idea to repeat some of the things we said about the skill of running itself. In running, the weight is transferred from one foot to the other. When we compare walking with running, the weight is transferred with a great deal more speed. The ball of the foot touches the ground first, and the toes point straight ahead. There is a short time when the body is in the air with no contact with the ground. In walking there is always contact with the ground with one of the feet.

In the run, there is more bending at the knees. This bending means lifting the legs higher. There is a higher arm lift and bending at the elbow. In running there is more of a body lean than in walking. The head points straight ahead.

The skill of running as we have described it applies much the same to baserunning. The big difference is that you will run only 55 feet in a straight line. Remember that 55 feet is the distance between bases. This distance is sometimes shortened for boys and girls at certain ages.

As soon as you hit the ball, the bat is dropped safely and you start the run to first base. If you see that you may only be able to get to first base, you should run "through" the base. If you decide that you can get more than one base, you will want to try for second base. In this case, you curve out to the right a few feet before you reach first base. In order to curve out you must slow down your run. You touch your foot on the inside of the base so that you will not run wide at the base.

When you are a baserunner waiting on base you lean forward with the left foot on the base. You should then be ready to push off quickly with the right foot when the ball is let go by the pitcher. Be sure you learn the proper skill of running before you apply it to baserunning.

PLAYING THE DIFFERENT POSITIONS

In just about every team sport most members of both teams are all active at the same time. This is not the case in softball. The batting team has one player at bat. It can have no more than three players on base. This means that at any one time the *offensive* team can have as many as four players and as few as one player active.

The fielding team or *defensive* team has nine of its players ready for action. At least they should be. Many times beginners in the game of softball do not do well because they are not sure what they are supposed to do in their positions. For this reason, we want to explain what each player is supposed to do in the position he plays.

Catcher

1. He stands behind the batter in a knee-bend position.
2. He holds the glove as a target for the pitcher.
3. He fields balls that are hit close to home plate. Many times he will be the one to field a bunted ball.
4. When there is not a baserunner on first base he backs up the first baseman. This means that when the ball is hit he runs down behind first base in case the first baseman misses the ball when it is thrown to him.

Pitcher

1. He becomes a fielder when the ball is hit close to him.
2. When the first baseman is off base fielding a ball, the pitcher covers first base.
3. When there is a runner on first base, he backs up the third baseman. Can you give a reason for his backing up the third baseman?
4. When there is a runner on second base, he backs up the catcher. Can you give a reason for his backing up the catcher?
5. Covers home plate when for some reason the catcher is drawn out of position.

First Baseman

1. He plays 8 to 10 feet off first base when there is no base-runner on the base and plays close to the base when there is a baserunner on first base.
2. He fields balls that are hit or thrown around the area of first base.
3. When there is not a baserunner on first base, he backs up the second baseman when throws come in from left field and

center field.

Second Baseman

1. He plays between first base and second base and stands about 8 to 10 feet back of the base line and about the same distance from second base.
2. He fields balls that are hit on the left side of second base.
3. When a ball is hit to the right side of second base, he covers the base to receive the ball fielded by another player.
4. He covers second base when the ball is thrown by the catcher.
5. He goes out to receive the ball from center fielder or right fielder and throws it to the infield.

Shortstop

1. He plays about half way between second base and third base and stands about 8 to 10 feet back of the baseline.
2. He fields the balls that go between second base and third base.
3. When a ball is hit on the first base side of second base, he covers second base.
4. On balls thrown from catcher, he backs up second baseman.
5. He goes out to receive the ball from left fielder and throws it into the infield.

Third Baseman

1. He plays about 6 to 8 feet off third base and stands about 3 or 4 feet back of the baseline.
2. He fields balls hit on the left side of the field and has to work closely with the second baseman in fielding balls.
3. On high fly balls around home plate, he sometimes comes in close to the catcher. If the catcher misses the ball he can sometimes recover it before it hits the ground.

Left Fielder

1. When balls are hit to the center field, he backs up the center

fielder.
2. When he sees that it is necessary he backs up the third
baseman. Can you think of any times when it would be
necessary for him to back up the third baseman?

Center Fielder

1. When a ball is hit to right field he backs up the right fielder.
2. When a ball is hit to left field he backs up the left fielder.
3. When a ground ball is hit to the shortstop or second
baseman he backs them up.
4. He backs up the second baseman on just about all plays that
come that way.

Right Fielder

1. He is the backup for the center fielder, second baseman, and
first baseman.
2. When a play is made at first base or second base, he backs it
up.

TEAM PLAY

Offensive team play and *defensive* in softball are somewhat
different than in most other games. This is certainly true of
offensive team play in softball. While there is some chance for a
batter and baserunner to work together, there are not a whole
lot of ways where this can happen. So when we talk about
offensive team play in softball we are really talking about indi-
vidual play. The following are some things to think about in
offensive play:

1. Be sure to "run out" all hits. It may look like an easy out,
but it is just possible that the first baseman will drop the
ball. If you have run out the hit you are more likely to be
safe at first than if you did not.
2. Run as fast as you can and overrun first base.
3. Be sure you know how many outs have been made if you
are on base.
4. Try to be a place hitter; try to hit the ball where the
fielders are not playing.

The following are some things to remember about defensive play:

1. Know where you should be playing in your position.
2. Know who you should back up when a play is made.
3. Think ahead about what you are going to do with the ball if it is hit to you. This means that you need to know the number of outs and players on base.
4. Try to make the play on a player who is closest to a score, that is, if a player is running for home try to get that player out.
5. Throw the ball to the base where the baserunner is going.
6. Talk to each other on the field so that each of you is sure what to do.

GAMES TO PRACTICE SOFTBALL SKILLS

Most of the old neighborhood games are baseball type games. You probably have played many of them at one time or another. The following games have been found useful by many boys and girls for practicing several of the skills required in softball.

Bases on Balls

This game is played on a softball diamond. You can use any distance you wish between the bases. There are two teams of any number on each team. One team is in the field while the other is at bat. A tennis ball or rubber playground ball can be used. The batter throws the ball up as in fungo batting and hits it with his hand into the field. The player in the field who gets the ball runs and places the ball on home plate. The batter runs the bases after he hits the ball. He gets a point for every base touched before the fielder places the ball on home plate. There are no outs in this game, and every player gets a chance to bat. When all players on a team have had a chance at bat, the teams change places. As many innings as desired can be played.

Hit Pin Baseball

This game is like softball except that objects such as bowling pins or empty milk cartons are used rather than bases. The pitcher throws the ball in easily so that the batter can hit it. When the batter hits the ball he starts around the bases. The fielder who gets the ball throws it to first base. The first baseman knocks the object over with the ball and throws the ball to second base. The game goes on until the ball has gone around all the bases and the objects have been knocked down. The batter scores one point for his team for every base he reaches before the object has been knocked down. The batter stops when the object (base) he is headed for is knocked down. There are no outs, and every member of the team gets to bat in each inning.

Base Run

There are four players on a team in this game. These players are a catcher, first baseman, second baseman, and third baseman. The catcher stands at home base, and the basemen are on their bases. There is a runner who tries to get around the bases once while the ball goes around twice. The runner starts when the catcher throws the ball to first. The first baseman throws the ball to second, and so on. The baserunner tries to beat the ball. If the runner gets around once before the ball gets around twice he scores one point for his team. After the four runners have had a chance to run, they become the basemen.

Beatball Softball

This game can have seven or more players on each team. If the batter hits the pitch he runs to first, second, third, and home without stopping. The fielders get the ball to the first baseman, who must touch the base with the ball in his hands. The first baseman throws the ball to the second baseman on base. The second baseman throws to the third baseman on base. The third baseman throws to the catcher. If the ball gets home before the runner, then he is out. The ball must beat the runner home and not just the bases ahead of the runner. If the runner beats the ball home he scores a run for his team. All of the other rules of softball apply.

Flies and Grounders

Any number of players can play this game. There is one batter, and the other players go into the field. The batter fungo bats the ball into the field. The player closest to the ball can go for it, and he calls out "Mine!" If he catches it on the fly, it counts five points. If he catches it on first bounce from a fly, it counts three points. If he catches a grounder, it counts one point. When a player gets fifteen points, he becomes the batter.

One Old Cat

In this game there are only two bases: first base and home base. As many as desired can be on each team. The first batter fungo bats the ball and runs to first base and back. He must make a complete trip. If he makes a complete trip without being put out, he scores a run for his team. The runner is out if a fly ball is caught or a fielder touches the runner with the ball before he reaches home. When a team makes three outs, they change places.

Chapter 7

FLAG FOOTBALL

FLAG football grew out of the game of touch football. The game of touch football grew out of the game of American football. Many people did not have a chance to engage in the game of football. The reason was that it was a very expensive game to play. So much equipment was needed that the average person did not have enough money to pay for it. Touch football provided a game where all could play without much expense.

The big difference in the game of touch football and regular football is that in touch football you are *not* allowed to tackle. This makes the game of touch football much less dangerous to play. In touch football a player is stopped by being touched rather than by being tackled. Because touching sometimes resulted in a form of pushing, which could cause serious injury, flag football was introduced. This game is the same as touch football except that a cloth (flag) is tucked in at the back of the waist of a player. A player is stopped when a player from the other team pulls the flag loose from the waist. This action prevents injury, and at the same time there is no question that the person was stopped. For these reasons, the game of flag football is used most widely in schools today.

We know that many of you are interested in tackle football. We recommend flag football in its place because of the reasons given above. Many professional football players have said that they do not care to have their own children play the regular game of football until they are grown. The reason they feel this way is that the contact game of football can be harmful to children who are still growing. The skills of flag football are much the same, and you can get just as much enjoyment out of it. There are many important skills to be learned in flag football. We will talk about these skills in this chapter.

PASSING

One important thing to remember in flag football skills is the shape of the ball. In all other games the ball is round. The balls do come in different sizes, as you can see when you compare a basketball with a softball. Because the ball is oval shaped in flag football some of the skills may be a little bit harder to do.

There are two kinds of passes in flag football. One of these is the *forward* pass, and the other is the *lateral* pass.

Forward Pass

The first thing to think about in forward passing is how to grip the ball. The fingers of the throwing hand grip the lace behind the center of the ball. The fingers are spread over the laces and the thumb around the ball. The smaller your hand, the nearer the end of the ball it should be.

The pass is made with the overarm throwing pattern, which was explained in Chapter 3. If you are right-handed you can use your left hand to help hold the ball while you are gripping it with the right hand. The ball is brought back past the ear. The body turns a little away from the direction of the throw. There is a step forward with the left foot pointing in the direction of the target. The weight shifts from the right foot to the left foot. The elbow of the throwing arm moves forward. The forearm comes forward with a whipping action. Allow the ball to roll off the fingertips. The ball should be thrown a little ahead of the person who is to catch it. This is the receiver, and he should be moving. Here are some important things to remember when throwing a forward pass.

1. Be sure to point the left foot in the direction of the throw, if you are right handed. If you are left handed, your right foot will be pointed in the direction of the throw.
2. Grip the ball where it is most comfortable. You may have to grip it nearer the end if you have a small hand.
3. Keep your eye on the target or on the person who is to catch the ball.
4. Practice to see how far back past the ear you will need to bring the ball.

Figure 37. FORWARD PASS!

5. Let the ball roll off the fingers with a whipping motion.
6. Follow through and have your fingers pointing toward the target at the end of the throw.

Lateral Pass

A lateral pass is one that is thrown sideways. It can be done with one or both hands. When done with one hand, it is about the same as the únderarm throwing pattern. The one-handed lateral pass is not used much by boys and girls because the ball is hard to grip.

When throwing a two-handed lateral pass, you should get a firm grip on the ball with both hands. You may be running with the ball and carrying it under one arm. You decide you want to make a lateral pass to a teammate. The ball is shifted from the one-arm carry to both hands. The ball is then shifted to the side of the body opposite the throw. You bring the ball across the body and let it go about waist high.

CATCHING

In flag football, catching is thought of as *receiving*. Those players whose main purpose is to catch the ball are called receivers. There are about three ways a ball may be caught or received in flag football: (1) catching while stationary, (2) catching a pass, and (3) catching a kicked ball.

Catching While Stationary

Usually a receiver will catch the ball while running. Sometimes the ball will not get to him. When that happens, he must stop and wait for the ball.

One foot is slightly ahead of the other. The feet are spread in a comfortable position. The arms and hands are extended toward the person who is passing the ball. The fingers are spread, and the hands are made into a cup.

As the ball comes toward the receiver, he transfers his weight to the foot that steps toward the ball. If the pass is high, the arms and hands move upward. The hands form a cup. When the ball is thrown low, the arms and hands move downward. The little fingers are together, and the hands again form a cup. The receiver gives with the ball when he contacts it. After the ball is caught, one end of it is placed under the arm above the elbow. The other hand is over the other end of the ball. You are now in a position to run with the ball.

Catching a Pass

Catching a forward pass is a very difficult skill. Because the receiver catches it while running, this kind of pass requires

Figure 38. CATCHING THE FORWARD PASS!

good timing and balance.

You should consider again the skill of running as explained in Chapter 1. After good running skill is accomplished, the receiver is better prepared to catch a forward pass.

The body weight is forward in the running position as the ball comes in. The arms and hands move upward to make the catch. The receiver looks over his shoulder at the passer and/or the ball. The arms and fingers are extended above the shoulders. The palms of the hands face the ball. The little fingers are together, and the hands form a cup. When you get control of the ball, bring it down to carrying position. Place one end of the ball above the elbow and the other hand over the other end of the ball.

Catching a Kicked Ball

There are two conditions when a player may be required to catch a kicked ball. One of these is when a ball is kicked off to start the game or after a score. The other is when the ball is punted by the other team. When a ball is kicked off, it will usually come in end over end. When it is punted, it will probably come in as a spiral, as in a forward pass. (However, a punt could come in end over end if it has not been punted well.) Even though the kicked ball can approach you in either of these ways, the way to catch it is about the same.

Try to get into a position where you think the ball will come down. This means you try to get lined up with the ball. The hands and arms are extended outward to form a "basket." Make sure you have the weight even on both feet. In the catching action, the fingers are spread apart forming a cup. The palms are upward. When you contact the ball, give with the hands and arms. Pull the ball in toward the middle of the body. As soon as you are sure you have control of the ball, place it under the arm and start running.

CARRYING THE BALL

In running with the ball you lean forward applying your best running skill. One end of the ball is placed under the arm and next to the body. There is a firm hand grip over the other end of the ball. This means that you make a cradle with the arm so that the ball will not fall out. When you first start to run with the ball, take short fast steps. Keep your knees high to be able to change direction. Remember to use the skill of dodging explained in Chapter 2. It is very important for a ball carrier to be able to know how to dodge well. When you are carrying the ball in an open field, take longer strides so that you can get more speed.

CENTERING THE BALL

Centering the ball is the way a play is started in flag football. The player who is the center passes the ball to one of the players in the backfield.

Figure 39. CENTERING!

In the starting position the center crouches down over the ball. The legs are spread, and one foot is a little bit behind the other. The knees are bent, and the weight is even on both feet. The right hand is placed over the front half of the ball. The left hand is on the back half of the ball. The thumbs are on top, and the fingers are on the side. The hips are about even with the shoulders.

Just before centering the ball, the body weight moves forward toward the toes. Very little weight is on the ball. The ball is passed back with both hands between the legs. The right hand passes the ball, and the left hand guides it. After the ball is let go, the center steps forward with the back foot. He is then ready to move forward.

PUNTING

The form of punting in flag football is about the same as for punting in the game of soccer. One thing to remember is that the ball is a different shape. For this reason, the ball might be harder to kick.

Figure 40. PUNTING!

In the starting position the kicker stands straight with the weight on the back foot. The arms are out in front, and both hands hold the ball. The left hand is on the left side of the ball near the front. The right hand is on the right side of the ball near the back. The front part of the ball is turned a little to the left.

There is a step forward with the left foot. Next there is a step with the right foot. Then there is another step with the left foot. The arms and the ball stay in the same position during the steps. Be sure to keep your eyes on the ball. Remember that the body weight is on the foot *not* used for kicking. If you are a right-footed kicker, the weight is on the left foot.

When the kicking leg comes forward, the ball is let go with both hands. The ball is kicked with the top of the foot. The toes are pointed in the direction of the kick.

STANCE

Stance means the position a player takes before play starts. This starting position can be either a three-point stance or a four-point stance.

In the three-point stance the feet are about shoulder width apart. One foot can be slightly ahead of the other. The player takes a crouch position with the knees bent. The weight is slightly forward and resting mostly on the knuckles of one hand. The reason it is called the three-point stance is that you are on both feet and the knuckles of one hand. The head should be up with the eyes looking straight ahead. You can move very quickly from this position.

In the four-point stance, the weight is on both feet and the knuckles of both hands. Everything else is the same as the three-point stance. You can use either of these stances. The stance you choose depends on where you are playing, on the line or in the backfield. Usually the backfield and linemen will use the three-point stance on offense. The four-point stance is used mainly by linemen on defense. The main thing, of course, is to get into the stance that is most comfortable for you.

BLOCKING

Blocking in flag football means that you get your body in front of a player on the other team. You try to block his path and not let him get to the ball. Most rules for flag football do not allow any kind of body contact. This means that you cannot push with your hands, shoulders, or hips in blocking a member of the other team. What you try to do is to get between the player and the ball without making body contact.

TEAM PLAY

There are many different sets of rules for flag football. Sometimes boys and girls like to make up their own rules on how they are going to play the game. Usually there are nine players on a team. Four of these are in the backfield, and five are on the line. However, there can be more or less players if so desired.

There are several things to keep in mind in offensive and defensive play in flag football. The following are some of the things you will want to remember about offensive play:

1. Be sure you know what you are supposed to do on each play.
2. Do not give away the play. Use the same stance each time you line up.
3. Remember the right carrying position when you are carrying the ball.
4. Practice the skills of dodging so that you will be better at carrying the ball.
5. If you are a receiver, use both hands to catch the ball.

The following are some things to remember about defensive play:

1. When you are defending against a pass receiver, try not to let him get behind you. It might be a good idea to practice the skill of galloping both forward and backward. This practice can help you change direction quickly when defending against a receiver. The skill of galloping was explained in Chapter 1.
2. Watch the ball and try to intercept it.
3. If you are a lineman keep your eyes on the ball. Watching the ball will help you follow the person carrying the ball.
4. If you are defending against a pass, you must try to watch both the passer and the ball.

5. When the passer lets the ball go, watch the ball and follow it.
6. Be sure you are close enough to the ball carrier to pull out the flag. If you are not close enough to reach out, you might miss the flag.

GAMES TO PRACTICE FLAG FOOTBALL SKILLS

Football Keep Away

Two or more teams with any number of players can play this game. Play starts with one of the teams' having the ball. This team passes the ball around to its own players. All other teams try to get the ball. When one of the teams intercepts the ball, that team gets it and tries to pass it around and keep it from the other teams. This game helps players develop the skill of handling the oval-shaped football.

Leader Ball Center Relay

Four or more players can play this game. One player is selected to be the leader. He stands with his back to the other players, who are standing in a line. The leader centers the ball to each member of the group. They return the ball to the leader. When a player misses the ball, he goes to the foot of the line. If the leader misses, he goes to the foot of the line, and the player at the head of the line replaces the leader. If desired, there can be several groups playing the game at the same time. The idea of this game is to practice the skill of centering the ball.

Football Kickball

This game requires two teams with any number on each team. The game is played on a softball diamond. All of the rules of softball are used. The ball is kicked instead of batted. The kicker stands at home plate and punts the ball. He runs to first base if the ball lands fair. All other rules of softball are used for the game. The idea of the game is to practice punting but at the same time make a game of it.

Football Zig-Zag

There are two teams of any number of players. Each team forms a line that faces the other team. The player at one end of the line starts the game by passing to a teammate across from him. The player passes the ball back, and so on. The game goes on until the ball gets to the last player in the line. The first team to get the ball back to the leader wins. The purpose of this game is to practice the skill of forward passing.

Teacher Football

Any number can play this game. It is probably best not to have more than five or six players. In this way the game goes faster, and the players get more turns. One player is selected to be the "teacher." The other players form a line facing the teacher. The teacher passes the ball to anyone in the line. If the player drops the ball, he goes to the end of the line, and the rest of the players move up. If the teacher drops the ball he goes to the end of the line, and the player at the beginning of the line becomes the teacher.

Kick and Catch

Two teams are needed for this game. There can be any number on each team. One team stands on one side of the field, and the other team stands on the other side. The game starts with a player of one team punting the ball to the other team. The player of the other team who is closest to the ball tries to catch it. If he catches it, he kicks it back. If the player misses the catch, the other team gets a point. After a certain amount of time, the team with the most points wins the game. This game gives players a chance to practice the skill of punting and also the skill of catching a kicked ball.

Chapter 8

VOLLEYBALL

LIKE basketball, the game of volleyball got its start in the United States. It was invented in 1895, four years after the game of basketball got started. The game was invented by William Morgan while he was teaching at the YMCA in Holyoke, Massachusetts.

You may remember that basketball was started as an indoor game that could be used to fill in between the end of football season in the fall and baseball season in the spring. It is believed that Mr. Morgan started the game of volleyball for those who were not interested in playing basketball.

Today, volleyball is one of the world's leading sports. One of the reasons for its popularity is that it is a game that can be played by people of all ages. Young and old alike seem to get a great deal of enjoyment out of hitting the ball back and forth across the net. It started out as an indoor game. Now it is played on playgrounds, in parks, on the beach, as well as many other places. Volleyball has become so popular that millions of people of all ages all over the world play the game. It has become one of the very important team sports in the Olympic Games.

The game got its name because the ball is volleyed back and forth across a net: the ball is hit with the hands. This action is called volleying. The idea of the game is to volley the ball back and forth with each team trying to score points. Points are scored by placing the ball in such a way that the other team cannot return it before it hits the floor.

The game is played on a court 60 feet in length by 30 feet in width. A net is placed over the middle of the court at a height of 8 feet (sometimes the net is lowered to 7 feet for women). The net can be placed at any height for boys and girls, depending on their age and skill. For beginners, a lightweight plastic ball or a beachball can be used to play the game.

There are six players on a team. Three of these are in the

front line, and three are in the back line. Players change their positions on the court at certain times during the game. This gives all players a chance to play in different positions in the front line and the back line. The ball can be hit three times by players on one team. The third person to hit it must get it over the net. One player cannot hit the ball two times in succession. It does not have to be hit three times, but it is best to do so. The reason for this is that it makes for better team play.

In 1971, the game of mini-volleyball was developed. This game is about the same as regular volleyball except that it is played on a smaller court. The net is usually 5 to 6 feet in height. There are three or four players on a side. In many places, boys and girls take part in mini-volleyball before they get into the game of regular volleyball. In many countries the beginning age for starting to play volleyball is nine years. It has been found that mini-volleyball is best for boys and girls of this age.

VOLLEYING

We have already said that volleying means that you hit the ball with your hands. Sometimes volleying is called passing because it is the way the ball is passed from one player to another and over the net. Remember that we said the ball should be volleyed and not caught. However, for beginners it is a good idea to catch the ball and throw it back and forth. The main thing is that the ball not be held too long after it is caught. You should let it go as quickly as possible. You let it go more quickly each time. Before long you will be able to volley the ball. You will find that it will be easier to volley the ball if you start out by throwing it. Sometimes for beginners the rules allow for the ball to bounce one time before it is volleyed. This is easier for some boys and girls than it is to hit the ball on the fly.

There are three kinds of volleys that we will talk about here: (1) overhead volley, (2) underhand volley, and (3) forearm volley.

Figure 41. OVERHEAD VOLLEY!

Overhead Volley

Some people consider the overhead volley the most important volleyball skill for boys and girls to learn. The reason for its importance is that it is the volleying skill that is probably used the most. It is used whenever the ball comes in chest high or higher. It is a difficult skill and takes a lot of practice.

The hands are held at about the level of the eyes. The fingers are spread with the thumbs almost touching each other. A little window is formed between the thumbs. The elbows are bent and out at about the height of the shoulders. The player takes a crouch position so that the ball will come in toward the eyes. The knees are bent enough to be in a comfortable position: one foot should be slightly ahead of the other. When the ball is contacted with the fingers and thumbs, the weight should be even on the balls of the feet. You strike the ball upward in the direction you are aiming. This will most likely be to a teammate if you are the first or second person to volley the ball. Try to volley the ball as high as 12 to 15 feet from the floor. Sometimes beginners make certain mistakes in the overhead volley. The following are these mistakes:

1. The ball is slapped rather than pushed.
2. The ball is hit more forward rather than upward.
3. The body is straight when the ball is hit rather than in a crouch.
4. Using one hand instead of both.
5. The player fails to get lined up with the ball.

If you can keep from making these mistakes when using the overhead volley, you will be more successful with it. Try to remember to keep your eyes on the ball, keep the knees bent, keep the elbows bent and shoulder high, and hit the ball high.

Underhand Volley

The underhand volley is no longer used in the game of volleyball. However, it is good to practice before trying the forearm volley. The knees are bent with the feet apart. The hands are below the waist with the palms facing inward. The fingers point downward with the little fingers together. The eyes are watching the ball. When the ball is contacted, the body weight is even on the balls of the feet. With the hands together you strike the ball upward. The arms, body, and legs are extended. The movement is completed by following through with the arms and body in the direction of the ball to finish the volley.

Figure 42. UNDERHAND VOLLEY!

Forearm Volley

The forearm volley is also called the *bump* or the *dig*. This volley is used mainly for four kinds of plays: (1) when the ball is low and below the waist, (2) to receive most serves, (3) to recover the ball off the net, and (4) when the player's back is

Figure 43. FOREARM BOUNCE VOLLEY! (BUMP)

toward the net.

One of the first things to consider in the forearm volley is the position of the hands. One hand is placed in the palm of the other hand. The thumbs are on top, and one thumb is placed over the other. The forearms are very close together. The body is in line with the ball, and the knees are bent. One foot can be slightly ahead of the other. The arms are lowered to prepare to receive the ball. The ball should bounce off the inside of the forearms and wrists. At the time the ball contacts the forearms it should be allowed to bounce rather than be met hard with the forearms. When contact is made with the ball, the body moves a little in the direction of the ball. It is a good idea to try to keep the ball high in the air.

SERVING

Serving is the way the ball is put into play. It means that the ball is hit with the hand by the player who is the server. The server is allowed to serve the ball from either the underhand position or the overhand position. The hand may be open or closed. Boys and girls should begin with the underhand serve. After you have been able to serve well with the underhand serve, you might want to try the overhand serve. We have found that some boys and girls can do well with the overhand serve. Others have a hard time with it and prefer to stay with the underhand serve.

Underhand Serve

The player stands facing the net. The left foot is a little ahead of the right foot. If you are left-handed, you should have the right foot ahead. The weight is on the rear foot. The body bends slightly forward. The ball is held in the left hand. It is in front and a little to the right of the body: the right hand should be lined up with the ball.

The serving motion is the same as the underarm throwing pattern explained in Chapter 3. The right arm swings forward and contacts the ball just below the center of it. Remember that the ball can be hit with the open hand or with the fist. If hit with the open hand, it should be with the heel of the fist. This means that the hand forms a fist with the thumb and index finger upward. To complete the serve you should follow through with the arm in the path of the ball. You can also step forward with the right foot after the serve.

Overhand Serve

In the overhand serve the right-handed server stands with the left foot in front. The left side is turned slightly toward the net. The ball is held in the palm of the left hand. The ball is about chest high. The weight is equal on both feet. The eyes watch the ball. The ball is tossed up two or three feet into the air. It is tossed above the right shoulder. When the toss is made, the weight shifts to the back foot. When the ball begins to drop, the weight is shifted to the forward foot. The arm is snapped forward, and the ball is contacted about a foot above the shoulder. The contact is made near the center of the ball with the tips of the fingers or fist. The overhead serving action is about the same as the overarm throwing pattern used to throw a softball.

THE SET

The set means that the ball is set up for a teammate to hit it over the net. Remember that a team is allowed to hit the ball three times. The set is usually the second hit. The ball is set up high for a teammate to spike it downward over the net. In setting up the ball, the overhead volley is used. The ball should be volleyed up at a height of about 12 to 15 feet. It is set up about one foot away from the net.

THE SPIKE

A spike means that the ball is hit downward as it goes into the other team's side of the court. It is a very important scoring skill, but it is very hard to learn. The player who is going to spike the ball stands close to the net. He faces the direction from where the ball is coming. When the ball starts to come

Figure 44. SPIKE!

down the spiker jumps high off the floor. He swings his right arm upward. He tries to hit the ball downward while it is still above the net. He should try to hit the ball on the top to get more force behind it. The spiker lands facing the net. He should be sure not to let his hand go over the net. As we said before, this skill is very difficult to learn. It is a good idea to practice spiking the ball with the net down fairly low.

THE BLOCK

The block is used against a spike. The player who is going to try to block the spike faces the net. He tries to jump at the same time the spiker does. He swings both arms upward with the hands close together. He should try to get about 6 inches above the net. If the blocker is successful, the ball will bounce off his hands and back into the other team's side of the court. Probably the hardest part about this skill is learning to jump just at the right time.

NET RECOVERY

Sometimes one of your teammates will hit the ball into the net on your side of the court. A player tries to recover the ball so that it will not hit the floor. If there have been one or two hits, a player can hit the ball as it bounces off the net. He faces the net and watches closely when the ball is going to hit. He uses the forearm volley to try to get the ball up high.

TEAM PLAY

Volleyball is a game in which there is a very quick shift back and forth from offense to defense. This is because the ball goes back and forth across the net very quickly.

A team scores only on its own serve. This means that when your team serves and, after one or more volleys back and forth over the net, the ball lands on the other team's side, your team would score a point. If the ball lands on your side of the court there would be no score for the other team because they were not the serving team.

The following are several important things to remember about offensive play:

1. The server should try to place the ball in an open space. It is also a good idea to try to serve it near the end of the court and close to the side line.
2. Remember that the ball can be hit by three members of your team. It must go over the net on the third hit. There will be better team play when the three hits are taken.
3. A three-hit play might go as follows: the ball is received by a back-line player; his hit is the first one, and it goes to a front-line player; this player makes the second hit and sets it up for a teammate to spike it; and the third hit is the spike over the net. This three-hit play takes a lot of practice and teamwork.
4. It is not a good idea for the front-line players to play with their backs to the net. They should either face the net or turn the body only about halfway around.
5. Remember to try to volley the ball high.

The following are some of the important things to remember about defensive play:

1. Always try to keep your eyes on the ball.
2. Usually try to keep one foot ahead of the other with the weight equal on both feet.
3. Most of the time a serve will be received by a back-line player. This player should volley the ball to a front-line player.
4. Sometimes if the serve is short, it can be received by a front-line player. If you are on the front line and have to jump too high for the ball, let it go to a back-line player.
5. Just like in the game of softball, certain players back up other players in volleyball. The player at the right in the back line backs up the player at the right in the front line. The player in the center of the back line backs up the player in the center of the front line. The player at the left in the back line backs up the player at the left in the front line.
6. Call out "Mine" or "My ball" if you are going to take the

ball. Your calling out will help keep two teammates from running into each other to get the ball.

GAMES TO PRACTICE VOLLEYBALL SKILLS

We said before that there are six players on a regular volley-ball team. There are three players in the front line and three players in the back line. The three players in the front line are the right forward, center forward and left forward. The three players in the back line are the right back, center back, and left back. In the following games any number can play. In these games we do not always follow the regular rules of volleyball. The idea for these games is to learn certain skills that can help make you a better volleyball player.

Net Ball

Net ball is played about the same as volleyball except that the ball is thrown back and forth across the net. The purpose is to get the players used to getting the ball over the net. If a player drops the ball, it counts a point for the other team. There can be as few as one player on a side. It is better to have three or four players on each side.

Keep It Up

Two or more teams of players with three or four players on a team can play this game. Each team forms a circle. On a signal, each team starts to volley the ball. The players on a team volley it to each other. They can use any kind of volley to do this. Whenever one of the teams allows the ball to hit the ground, it counts a point against that team.

Serve Up

Two people can play this game, or more can play if desired. You serve the ball to your partner, and he serves it back. You start out with a short distance and then keep making the distance longer.

Volley Up

This game is the same as serve up except that you and your partner volley the ball back and forth rather than serving it back and forth. You try to see how many good volleys you can get without letting the ball hit the ground. You and your partner can play against another player and his partner.

Wall Volleyball

From two to four players can play this game. You will need a wall to bounce the ball against. The idea of the game is to keep the ball bouncing against the wall. One player starts by serving against the wall. It is returned by the next player. Play goes on with the players taking turns hitting the ball. After the serve, the ball is volleyed against the wall. If a player allows the ball to hit the ground, the player who last hit the ball against the wall scores a point.

Volleyball Keep Away

Two teams with any number of players on a team can play this game. It is a good idea to have at least three players on a team. The team members try to volley the ball to each other. The other team tries to get the ball. If they do, they try to volley it to each other. The team that volleys the ball the greatest number of times wins the game. This is a good game to play with a beachball.

INDEX

111